The Story of the Christians

by Jennifer Rye

Illustrated by
Chris and Hilary Evans

Cambridge University Press

Cambridge
London   New York   New Rochelle
Melbourne   Sydney

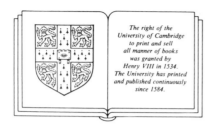

Published by the Press Syndicate of the University of Cambridge
The Pitt Building, Trumpington Street, Cambridge CB2 1RP
32 East 57th Street, New York, NY 10022, USA
10 Stamford Road, Oakleigh, Melbourne 3166, Australia

First published 1986

Printed in Great Britain

ISBN 0 521 301181 hard cover
ISBN 0 521 317487 paperback

The photographs reproduced in this book are with the
following permissions:

'Christ in Glory' tapestry, at Coventry Cathedral
    Nicholas Servian/Woodmansterne.

'The Resurrection', by Piero della Francesca, and
Michelangelo's Pietà: The Mansell Collection.

Typesetting: G & E

What is a Christian?

The Christian religion was started by the followers of Jesus Christ, who lived almost two thousand years ago. Christianity, as it is called, grew out of the Jewish religion. It started in the Middle East and spread to become a world religion. There are Christians in places as far apart as Iceland and India, Africa and Australia. Because Christians consider that a new era began with the birth of Jesus Christ, they work out all dates as BC (Before Christ) or AD (Anno Domini, meaning in the year of our Lord). This Christian way of dating events is now used by most countries.

So, what do Christians believe? What have they in common with the followers of other world religions and in what ways are they different?

Christians believe that Jesus Christ was, and is, the son of God. They believe that there is only one God and that he made the world and everything in it. They believe that because he is a loving God he sent his son Jesus into the world, as a human being, to help his fellow humans become perfect.

Jews and Muslims also believe in the same supreme God, but they think of Jesus just as a great prophet. It is only the Christians who think of him as the son of God. All Christians believe this, although many Christians disagree about other parts of their religion.

So Christians think of God as a Father, and also as a Son. They think of him in a third way too, as what they call the Holy Spirit. That makes three ways of looking at God, so Christians sometimes refer to God as the Trinity, a word which comes from the Latin word *tres*, meaning three.

Christians believe that, after the death of Jesus, God sent his spirit to help the new Christians to follow the example Jesus had given them in leading the sort of lives that God wants for them. According to Christian belief, Jesus died, as all humans do, but he then came to life again and will live for ever. They believe that the same thing will happen to them.

The life and teachings of Jesus

Jesus was born in a country called Judea, which two thousand years ago was part of the Roman Empire, but is now part of the modern state of Israel. His family, like everyone else in Judea, were Jews, and followed the ancient Jewish religion. The story of the Jews is told in the first part of the Bible, the Hebrew bible, which Christians call the Old Testament.

The second part of the Bible, the New Testament, tells the story of Jesus and the early Christians. The first four books, the Gospels, were probably written by men who had known Jesus, or who had collected the stories from other people who had known him. They were called Matthew, Mark, Luke and John.

In the Gospels by Matthew and Luke, we are told that Mary knew she was going to have a special baby. An angel called Gabriel had told her that God had chosen her to be the mother of his son. When it was nearly time for her baby to be born, an order came from the Roman Emperor that everyone had to be registered. So she and her husband, Joseph the Carpenter, had to leave their home in Nazareth, and go to Bethlehem to register. The town was so full that they could not find anywhere to stay, and they may have slept in a stable. Certainly, when her baby was born she put him to sleep in a manger. As the angel had told her to, she named him Jesus.

The hills around Bethlehem were sheep-farming country. Some shepherds who were sitting all night guarding their flocks from danger saw a new star in the sky, and heard an angel say that it was a sign of "the saviour, which is Christ the lord". They decided to follow the star. It shone over the place where Mary had just given birth to Jesus. The story also goes that there were others who visited the baby; these were astrologers, known as wise men, who had also followed the star. They gave presents to the new baby.

Nobody really knows much about Jesus as a boy. We think that he grew up working with Joseph in the carpenter's shop, back in their home in Nazareth. The Gospels tell his story again from when he left home at the age of about thirty, and spent three years travelling around his country. He shared the lives of the ordinary people, staying in their homes and making friends with them.

He became famous for healing people who were ill – just by touching them, although sometimes he did not want everyone to know about it. He gave sight to the blind, made deaf people hear again, and brought dead people back to life. These miracles made him well known and brought him lots of followers. To help him in his work of teaching and healing, he chose twelve men to be his special friends, his disciples.

It was not just the extraordinary things Jesus did that made him famous, it was what he said as well. He reminded the Jews that God is the father of everyone, and that therefore all men are brothers and should treat each other lovingly. He said, "Love your enemies, do good to those who hate you, bless those who curse you."

Jesus said he knew what God was like, because God was his father. This claim made a lot of Jews very angry. He seemed like a dangerous troublemaker, and the Jewish leaders were frightened of his influence. Their chief priests and the Roman governor in Jerusalem wanted to get rid of him. It was the time of the Jewish Passover so Jesus arranged to take the Passover supper with his disciples. He knew that it would be their last meal together. He told them that the bread they were eating was "my flesh" and the wine they were drinking was "my blood", to help them remember him after his death. So bread and wine are important to Christians, when they remember that last meal, in a service which is an important part of their faith.

After the 'Last Supper' Jesus was arrested and charged with the crime of claiming to be the son of God. Under Jewish law this crime was punishable by death. The Roman governor, Pontius Pilate, faced with the possibility of riots, reluctantly agreed to the death sentence. Jesus was executed on a hill outside Jerusalem by a method called crucifixion, common at the time. He was nailed by hands and feet to a cross, and left to die.

His dead body was then removed from the cross, and put into a tomb whose entrance was sealed by a large stone and guarded by Roman soldiers. But when his friends and disciples came to the tomb later, they found the stone rolled away and his body gone. Then they remembered – Jesus had told them he would rise from the dead. They were sure that this was what had happened.

The Gospels record that the disciples saw Jesus again some days later. He told them that he was going to join his father in heaven and that they should spread his teaching. He said that he would be with them always until the end of time, and that he would also send the Holy Spirit to help them.

So, the first Christians were those followers who had known Christ, setting out to tell the story of his life and to spread his teachings, as he had told them to.

The Resurrection painted by
Piero della Francesca (1416–1492)

The early years of Christianity

Soon after Jesus had left them the disciples were all together in Jerusalem. An amazing thing happened. A great wind blew through the house they were in and flames seemed to flicker over their heads. They found that they could speak different languages all at once. People who heard were utterly astonished, but the disciples knew that his was the coming of the Holy Spirit.

Even so, the first Christians did not find it easy to carry out the task which they had been set by Jesus. Their fellow Jews were shocked by the Christians' claim that Jesus was the son of God. When they started to preach to non-Jews, that made them even more unpopular. However, they did not give up.

A man called Paul became a great Christian leader and wrote many letters to groups of Christians in towns around the Mediterranean. They are in the New Testament. He addressed them to "the church at Ephesus", "the church at Corinth", and so on. The word 'church' meant the group of people who believed in Christ, and who met, secretly, in each other's houses to pray together.

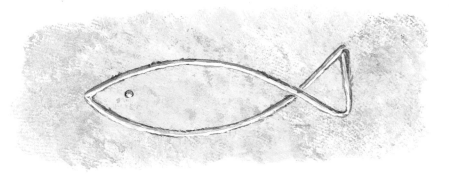

It was dangerous to be a Christian. They used a secret sign to recognise each other – it was a simple drawing of a fish. Many were tortured to make them give up their faith, and some were even killed. In spite of this, their numbers grew. After about three hundred years, the Roman Emperor Constantine himself became a Christian and then it became safer. Eventually they started to build churches where they could worship God. They used the shape of the cross on which Jesus died as a symbol of their belief that even death could not defeat Christians.

When the Roman Empire was split into two in 1054, the Christians finally divided into two main groups. The eastern part became the Orthodox Church centred on Constantinople, now known as Istanbul, in Turkey, and the western part became the Catholic Church, with its headquarters in Rome. The leader of the Catholic Church was the bishop of Rome, who was called the Pope. Under him were other bishops, and under them were the priests who served each church and its members. The Orthodox Church had a similar system, but without one central leader like the Pope.

Living the religious life

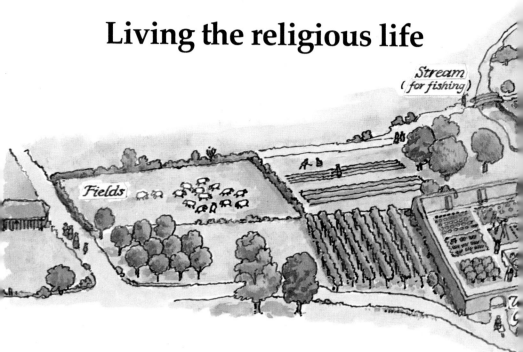

From the earliest times, some people have wanted to give their whole lives to their religion. The first Christian monks were men who chose to live alone in caves or remote huts, spending all their life in prayer. The word 'monk' comes from the Greek word *monos*, meaning alone.

Monasteries developed when groups of monks decided to share the religious life together. They lived according to strict rules which helped them to concentrate on God rather than on themselves.

Monasteries were for men. But of course there were women, too, who wanted to devote their whole lives to God. They became nuns, took the same vows as monks did, and lived in nunneries or convents.

Different kinds of monks and nuns belonged to different 'Orders' according to the rules they followed, and they specialized in different things. Some were famous for farming, like the Cistercians, who were very successful sheep farmers. Other Orders were well known for studying, or music, and their monasteries were great centres of learning and culture. For hundreds of years, in the so-called Dark Ages, it was the monks and nuns of Western Europe who kept scholarship alive.

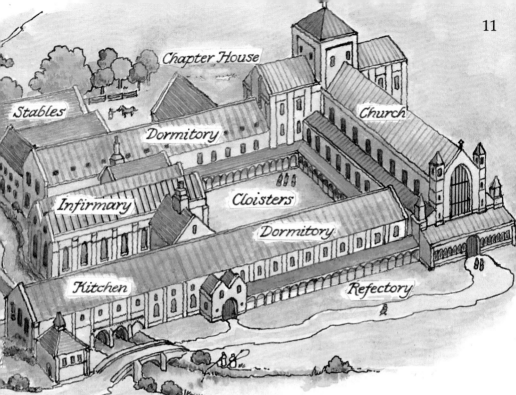

The buildings which the monks lived in were very fine. The community had to be self-sufficient – that is, it had to produce everything needed by the people who lived in it. All the buildings were grouped round the church, for the worship of God was their main concern. The chapter house and parlour were usually to the east of the church, with the dormitory above. This was linked to the church by a stair so that the monks could get there easily for prayers at night – services went on throughout the day and night. There were cloisters – a sort of sheltered courtyard for walking and reading with a garden in the middle – kitchen and refectory for meals, stables, smithies and barns grouped around. Beyond were the vegetable and fruit gardens and monastery lands.

There are still monks and nuns living in the same way today, worshipping God and serving others. Many work as teachers or nurses, but there are also some who spend all their lives praying and thinking about God. Nowadays they do not all wear the traditional long clothes of the early monks and nuns, and some live outside in the community instead of in monasteries or convents.

A few famous Christians

Saint Columba (born 521, died 597)
An Irish monk, who founded many monasteries, the most important being Iona, on an island off the west coast of Scotland. Through his teaching, his example and the miracles he did, he converted many heathens to Christianity.

**The Venerable Bede
(born about 673, died 735)**
He was a Benedictine monk, famous as the first English historian. He wrote the 'Ecclesiastical History of the English Nation', and many other books about science and religion as well as history.

Saint Francis (born 1182, died 1226)
Born into a rich Italian family, he rejected their comfortable life and became a poor wandering friar. He is well known for his love of animals and nature. He founded an order of monks, called the Franciscans, and laid great stress on their vow of poverty.

Elizabeth Fry (born 1780, died 1845)
A Quaker from East Anglia, who devoted her life to improving conditions in nineteenth century prisons, particularly for women. A Quaker is a member of the Society of Friends, who have taken a leading part in many social reforms.

General William Booth
(born 1829, died 1912)
Originally a Methodist, he organised a number of missions to the poorest people in the industrial towns of England. The most successful of these was the Salvation Army: they aim to bring Christianity to people whom the churches do not reach.

Saint Bernadette
(born 1844, died 1879)
Bernadette Soubirous was a French peasant girl, from Lourdes. She saw visions of the Virgin Mary in a cave by the river in her home town. Lourdes has since become a centre of pilgrimage, especially for sick and crippled people. Some miraculous cures have happened there.

Mother Teresa
(born 1910 – still living)
She is a Roman Catholic missionary, noted for her work among the homeless and starving in Calcutta, India. Her original name was Agnes Gonxh Bojaxhiu, and she was born in Yugoslavia, but she is now known throughout the world as 'Mother Teresa of Calcutta'.

Martin Luther King
(born 1929, died 1968)
American clergyman and civil rights leader. He is famous for leading non-violent action against the policy of separating black and white people in the southern states of America. He won the Nobel peace prize in 1964 and was murdered four years later.

The Crusades

The city of Jerusalem has always been an important place for Christians, ever since Jesus was crucified there. In the Middle Ages they called it the Holy City, and many pilgrims made the long journey from Europe to visit Jerusalem and pray there.

Jerusalem was a holy city for people of other religions too, for the Jews of course, and also for the followers of the Prophet Muhammad, the Muslims. The city was controlled by the Muslims from the 7th century onwards, and at first they allowed Christians to visit and pray there. But in the 11th century a new group of Muslims from Turkey took control of the eastern end of the Mediterranean. They closed not only Jerusalem to Christians, but also the Christian centre of the Orthodox Church, Constantinople.

For the next two hundred years there was war in that area between Christians and Muslims. These wars were called 'the Crusades' by Christians. The cross of Christ was the sign of the Crusades, worn on their clothes and armour; (the word 'crusade' comes from the French *croix*, meaning a 'cross'.) Although the Muslims and Christians believed in the same God, they had different ways of worshipping him, and at that time the differences seemed more important than anything else. So Christians went out to kill others in the name of their God of love!

Some of the knights who joined the Crusades were looking for riches or lands for themselves, not really caring much about the Holy City. They even attacked the Christian city of Constantinople themselves, set fire to it, and stole many treasures.

Although the Crusaders were successful in some battles, and captured Jerusalem in 1099, the Muslims had won it back within one hundred years. Some Crusaders settled in the Holy Land, and set up a new Christian kingdom there called *Outremer* – the kingdom beyond the sea. To protect their lands, they built impressive castles all along the coast, which are still there today. Two special orders of fighting monks were started, to guard the pilgrim routes and to look after the travellers. They were called the Knights of St John and the Knights Templar.

By the end of the 13th century, the Muslims had won back all their land from the Christians, Outremer was ended, and the holy war was over. It left only misunderstanding and bad feeling between some Christians and Muslims. This war did not achieve much for either side.

The clash of ideas

When Constantinople was conquered by the Muslims in 1453, the Eastern Orthodox Church moved its headquarters to Russia. The Catholic Church continued with its centre in Rome, and its language Latin. It became a very powerful force in medieval Europe, and the Pope was more powerful than many kings.

But as the church became more and more powerful, some people believed that it had moved away from the simple ideals that Jesus had taught. They wanted to be free from its control, free to choose their own ways of worshipping.

In the 16th century, a German monk called Martin Luther declared that the Church must be reformed to bring it back to true Christianity. The Pope did not agree, and although he insisted he was still a Catholic, Luther started a new way of worshipping. He used the German language for services instead of Latin, so that people could understand them and not need a priest to translate for them. He translated the Bible into German too.

In England, King Henry VIII broke off the English Church from Rome and made it independent. Although

the English Church kept many Catholic beliefs, the King was head of it instead of the Pope. The monarch is still head of the Church of England today.

Once one group of protesters had challenged the power of the Catholic Church, and been successful, it was easier for others to do the same. The new Churches were still Christian, of course, and members of each Church thought that they alone had the right way of worshipping. They were all sure that all the others were wrong.

These new ideas of reform, which were common all over Europe in the 16th and 17th centuries, have been given the name of 'the Reformation'. The people who protested at what they thought was wrong with the Catholic Church were called Protestants. The new independent churches that they set up are called the protestant churches. So this was the second split amongst the Christians: first Orthodox and Catholics, now Catholic and Protestants. Once again, as had happened in the Crusades, people who worshipped the same God but did so in different ways, argued and fought with one another, and ever tortured each other in their attempts to prove that they were right.

Luther pins up a poster to declare his beliefs

More new ideas

The Roman Catholic church remained in control of most of southern Europe, countries like Italy and Spain, which are still mostly Catholic countries today. In northern Europe, though, many new Protestant churches grew up. Often a new church was founded by one man who liked to think things out for himself.

One of these men was John Calvin. He preached his new ideas in France, but so many people there disagreed with him that he had to move to Switzerland, where he founded a new church. John Knox brought Calvin's ideas to Scotland, and his followers there founded the Presbyterian church. 'Presbyter' means an older man, and in that church it is 'the elders' among the members who are elected to run it.

Ever since the time of Luther, groups of Protestant Christians have started their own churches, according to their own beliefs. The names of these churches come sometimes from their customs, as with the Baptists, who stress the importance of baptism. Each person being accepted as a full member of their church has to be

Inside a Baptist chapel

baptised in a special pool that they have in each chapel, and is completely covered with water, or immersed. This is how Jesus was baptised in the river Jordan, in Judea.

As a rule, Protestant churches are plainer than Catholic ones, with less decoration. Services are held in the everyday language of the people, so that everyone can understand. The Bible is in their language too, so that everyone can read it for themselves. Catholics, until recently, used Latin as their language of worship, but now they too usually use the language of the countries they live in.

Other names that are given to the protestant churches are 'reformed' and 'nonconformist'. To conform means to accept, so Nonconformists are people who did not accept the old rules but made their own new ones. There are now two hundred and fifty different Christian churches, each with its own rules and beliefs. Some, like the Roman Catholic Church, have millions of members. Others have only hundreds.

Christianity spreads worldwide

As the people of Europe explored the rest of the world, they took their religious ideas with them. In fact, spreading their religion was often one of the reasons for their voyages of exploration.

In 1492 Christopher Columbus set off from Spain to explore westwards. Many more explorers and adventurers, hungry for land and riches, followed him and claimed large areas of central and South America for Spain. They forced most of the people who were already living there to become Catholics. Parts of North America, especially what is now Canada, were settled by French Catholics. The Indians who lived there were persuaded to become Catholics too.

The 'Mayflower' sights land

Some English Protestants left their country in 1620 to start a new life in America. They were called the Pilgrim Fathers. They left to get away from the Church of England so that they could live and worship God in the way they wanted, a way they thought was purer than that of the church at home. They founded new Puritan churches in the land they called New England.

Other groups of people started different kinds of Protestant churches in North America. Gradually the number of Christians in North and South America grew. Different groups of Christians founded new churches so that they could worship in their own way.

In the nineteenth century, many of the Christian churches sent missionaries abroad to tell people about Jesus Christ. They went all over the world, to India, Africa, China and Japan. They wanted to help the people who lived in those countries, so they went as teachers, nurses and doctors as well as explorers. They founded schools and built hospitals as well as churches. These missionaries were trying to do what Jesus had done – care for the sick and handicapped, and also preach the word of God. Today some people think that these 19th century missionaries tried to impose too many European ideas – not just religious ones – on the people they were trying to help.

And so Christianity, which had begun in Judea, a small province of the Roman Empire at the eastern end of the Mediterranean, with a small number of Jewish people who knew and followed a man called Jesus of Nazareth, had by the beginning of the twentieth century, spread over the whole world. In every country you could find Christians.

Christian rituals and services

Although all Christians share the belief that Jesus is the son of God, they have many different Churches all over the world and different ways of worshipping.

Christian services have three main purposes. Firstly, Christians join together in worshipping and praising God. They also pray to God and ask him for help, both for themselves in trying to lead a Christian life, and for others who are suffering in various ways. Thirdly, they need to learn about their own faith, so some services are in the form of instruction or teaching. Most services combine all these aims.

These aims are part of what individual Christians should do on their own. But in joining together in church services to praise God, pray to him, and learn more about him, they share these common aims, and help one another to be better Christians.

The most important service for the majority of Christians is the Mass, which is also called the Eucharist or the Lord's Supper. In the Mass, Christians remember the Last Supper of bread and wine which Jesus shared with his disciples before he was taken prisoner and crucified. Sharing bread and wine in the Mass is the way that Christians share in the life and sacrifice of Jesus.

Another important service for Christians is Baptism. A person becomes a Christian by being baptised – they are given a Christian name and welcomed into the world family of Christians. For their part, they have to declare that they believe in God, and promise to be a faithful follower of Jesus Christ. Often the new Christian is a baby, too young to make promises, so the parents and sponsors, called godparents, make the promises for the child.

Some church services are social occasions as well as being religious rituals. At a Christian wedding, the bride and bridegroom promise to be faithful to each other all their lives, and they make that promise to God. Their friends and relations are invited to the wedding to witness this vow, which is a legal contract between the two people getting married.

For a funeral there is another service at which religious and social life are mixed. Christians believe in the life after death, so dying for them is like opening a door into another life. But the family and friends will miss the dead person, so there is both joy and sorrow at a funeral. After the prayers, the coffin with the dead body inside is buried in a graveyard, or burned at a crematorium and ashes are buried or scattered. The burial place is marked with a stone or cross.

Christianity inspires the Arts

Artists of all kinds have been inspired by the Christian religion in the last two thousand years. Musicians, sculptors, painters, writers, wood-carvers, embroiderers and many other craftsmen have created great works of art which show Biblical scenes, or other subjects related to the Christian religion.

This was because works of art were mainly commissioned for churches, ordered and paid for either by church funds, or by a person who wanted to donate something to a church. So for several hundred years, many artists painted scenes from the stories in the Bible.

Michelangelo's *Pieta* sculpture

The Sistine Chapel in Rome, built at the end of the fifteenth century, is decorated all over the walls and ceiling with wonderful pictures showing the creation of the world by God, scenes from the life of Jesus, and the Last Judgement. The largest of these murals were painted by Michelangelo. He also carved a marble *Pietà* – Mary cradling the body of the dead Christ, which is one of the most famous statues in the world.

Great composers wrote pieces of music which are based on religious themes. 'The Messiah' by Handel, for example, is a very famous oratorio, a dramatic piece of music for soloists, chorus and orchestra, which tells the story of the life of Christ.

Monks in the Middle Ages copied out books by hand, and illustrated them with beautiful designs and pictures; these are now kept in museums and treasured as precious works of art.

Christ in Glory
by Graham Sutherland

The first printing presses were used to print Bibles. For nearly four hundred years the 'King James Bible', printed in England in 1611, has been read all over the world wherever English is spoken, and it is regarded as a masterpiece of English prose, a work of art in itself.

The religious themes and ideas which have inspired artists all through the centuries are still working on the creative imaginations of artists today. Coventry Cathedral, rebuilt since the second world war, and designed by Sir Basil Spence, is just one example. The great British composer, Benjamin Britten, was commissioned by Coventry to write a new work, and he produced the War Requiem which had its first performance in the new Cathedral. Graham Sutherland designed the huge tapestry *'Christ in Majesty'*, showing Christ sitting on his throne which hangs there.

Christian buildings

Only the cross on the roof shows that this is a Christian church in Manganeng, Transvaal, South Africa.

The parishes of England were once groups of settlements, each with its own church. Today, the parish church is used by members of the Church of England, or Anglicans. Most of these buildings are very old, and they are all different.

The first settlers in Massachusetts kept their religious beliefs firmly at the centre of their lives. The church building at Concord, New England, USA, is at the centre of the community. It is built in plain unadorned style that seemed right to those Puritan settlers.

St George's Church at Cape Drepanum, in Cyprus. It is built in the shape of a cross, with a central dome, like many Greek Orthodox churches.

The range of buildings inspired by Christianity and used by Christians throughout the world is amazing.

Catholic priests spread the Christian religion to the Indians in what is now California, and built missions like this one at San Carlos de Borromeo, in the United States of America.

A chapel is a centre of worship within a larger institution, such as a college or hospital or prison. King's College Chapel in Cambridge, England was begun in 1446 and completed in 1515, for use by the scholars of the college.

Building a medieval cathedral was an enormous task for everyone. The huge, towering, beautiful structures, built to declare the glory of God, often took hundreds of years to build. This is Chartres, in France.

Christian background to everyday life

For Christians whose religion is important to them, God is at the centre of each of their lives, which they try to base on the teachings of Jesus. But many people do not realise how much the Christian tradition affects us all every day, practising Christians or not.

The word holiday, which means holy day, is a reminder of the Christian year. Most of the important public holidays that we enjoy are based on events that Christians remember and celebrate as religious festivals.

Christmas is an obvious example. Christmas for most people now means eating and drinking more than usual, lots of parties and presents, cards and decorations, Christmas trees and crackers. Advertising for Christmas starts in September, encouraging people to spend lots of money on presents and food and drink. But Christmas means literally the mass of Christ. It is, for Christians, the celebration of the birth of the Christ child. On December 25th, Christians remember that God sent his son, Jesus Christ into a human family, and they go to church on that day to thank God for that great gift. The presents that we give to each other at Christmas are a reminder of the gifts brought to the stable by the three wise men.

Pancake day has another name – it is called Shrove Tuesday in the Christian church. It is the last day before Lent, which starts 6 weeks before Easter. In Lent, Christians remember Christ making himself strong by praying and going without food in the desert before he started his work of preaching and healing. Some Christians discipline themselves in the same way during Lent, making an extra effort to be good followers of Christ. In Catholic countries especially, there are great parties and carnivals before Lent begins. Pancakes are the feast before the fasting starts.

Easter is another holiday, when schools and shops and businesses are closed, so that friends and families may enjoy having free time together. But for Christians,

Easter is not just a holiday, it is the most holy day in the year. On Good Friday, they remember Christ's death on the cross. It is called "good", because unless he had died, he would not have been able to rise to a new life. On Easter Sunday, Christians celebrate Christ's rising from the dead, or resurrection.

All through the year, there are reminders that modern public 'holidays' come from the ancient 'holy days' of the Christian year.

Every Sunday is a special day for Christians, because the seventh day of the week was the day that Christ rose from the dead. It has also become a day of rest, part of the weekend when people have leisure time. The idea of a day of rest comes first from the Jewish, and then from the Christian tradition.

Whenever people live together in groups they work out rules for themselves which all the members of the group can agree to and accept. The rules accepted in Britain, for instance, originate in many countries, as different people settled in Britain, bringing their customs with them. Many of the ideals that the law now protects in Britain are Christian ones. Looking after less fortunate people in our society, and those who are sick and handicapped, is an aim which comes from the example Jesus gave.

The ideas and ideals of many modern countries have been very much influenced by Christian teachings. If Jesus Christ had never lived, or if the Christian religion had not spread from Judea all over the world, life in the twentieth century would have been quite different.

A Red Cross station in a Third World country

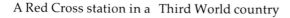

Christianity today

The story of the Christians is not finished yet. Nearly two thousand years have passed since Jesus was alive, and the number of his followers has grown and grown. In this century, the twentieth, there are still new chapters in the story.

Some of the splits that have appeared between different kinds of Christians are being closed. Various Protestant churches are finding ways in which they are alike, rather than concentrating on their differences. Catholics, Protestants and Orthodox Christians want to co-operate more with each other. Many people think it is wrong for Christians to be divided as they have been, and they are praying for unity in what is called the Ecumenical movement. The World Council of Churches was set up in 1948, so that all sorts of Christians could express one opinion on world affairs, but this has not always proved possible.

Some Christians think they should be trying harder to co-operate with non-Christians and followers of other religions. Christians, like other people, are trying to help the poor and disadvantaged in the world today, but many think that much more could and should be done to share the world's riches more fairly.

There are tremendous disagreements among Christians over questions like: Should women become priests? Should priests get involved in politics or revolution? Christians are undecided about whether they should support the arms race, or whether they should be pacifists, declaring that war is always wrong.

In spite of all these questions and arguments, Christianity is still a living, growing religion, changing to meet the needs of a changing world. For Christians there is only one certainty that does not change – that Jesus Christ, the son of God, came to save the world God made.

The Lord's Prayer

Our Father in heaven
hallowed be your name,
your kingdom come,
your will be done,
on earth as in heaven.
Give us today our daily bread.
Forgive us our sins
as we forgive those who sin against us.
Lead us not into temptation
but deliver us from evil.
For the kingdom, the power, and the glory
are yours
now and forever.

Amen.

One day, the disciples were watching Jesus pray. When he finished, they asked him to tell them the right way to pray to God.
Jesus replied with the words of The Lord's Prayer, which is used by all Christians.
It finishes, as many prayers do, with the word 'Amen', which means 'So be it'.